Mi Familia Me Importa
El ABC del Mejoramiento del Hogar

My Family
Matters To Me

The ABCs Of Home Improvement

By Dr. (Por la Dra.) Marlena E. Uhrik

Illustrated by (Ilustrado por) Minh Dang

ISBN 10: 0-97973682X
ISBN 13: 978-0979736827
Library of Congress Control Number: 2013949605

Original creative concept: Marlena E. Uhrik, Ed.D.

Special thanks to Spanish Professor and Hayward City Council member, J Francisco Zermeno C
(http://www.zermeno.com/Terlingua.htm) and his student Silvia Enriquez for the Spanish translation of My
Family Matters To Me.

-- Gracias especiales al profesor de español y Concejal de Hayward, J Francisco Zermeño
C (http://www.zermeno.com/Terlingua.htm) y a su estudiante Silvia Enríquez por la traducción en español
de Mi Familia me Importa.

A special acknowledgment goes to Lourdes Gonzalez-Peralta for her editorial contribution to the Spanish
version of this book and for making sure that my words and emotions were able to transcend cultures and
language.

Un agradecimiento especial a Lourdes González-Peralta por su contribución editorial a la versión en
español de este libro y por asegurarse que mis palabras y sentimientos pudieran trascender culturas y
lenguaje.

Designed and produced by
PUBLISHERS DESIGN GROUP, INC.
Roseville, California
www.publishersdesign.com

Published by
ALL WAYS LEARNING, LLC
Sacramento, California
www.allwayslearning.biz

Printed in USA

Thank You!!!

Special thanks to Carol Quint for the hours of editing and years of friendship.

Recognition also goes to friends and family who gave their support and for the original idea of this book: Aaron Edens, Wendy Ledward, Liz Edens, Chris Stone, Blake Grant, Donna White, Patti Hart, George and Jordan Leong, Pam Lowe, Carol Pugner, the kids at Woodrow Woods School in Hayward, California, and especially, my husband, Bill Wheelock.

Also, special recognition goes to our illustrator, Minh Dang and his charming characters, Cosmo and friends, who gave new life to *My Family Matters To Me*.

A special acknowledgment to Lourdes Gonzalez-Peralta for her editorial contribution to the Spanish version of this book and for making sure that my words and emotions were able to transcend cultures and language.

¡Gracias!

Un agradecimiento para Carol Quint por las horas que paso editando y por los años de amistad.

También envió un reconocimiento para mis amigos y familia que me dieron su apoyo y ayudaron con la idea original de este libro: Aaron Edens, Wendy Ledward, Liz Edens, Chris Stone, Blake Grant, Donna White, Patti Hart, Georgey Jordan Leong, Pam Lowe, Carol Pugner, los niños de la Escuela Woodrow Woods en Hayward, California, y especialmente, a mi esposo, Bill Wheelock.

También, un reconocimiento especial va para nuestro ilustrador, Minh Dang y sus bonitos personajes, Cosmo y sus amigos, quienes le dieron nueva vida a *Mi Familia Me Importa*.

Un agradecimiento especial a Lourdes González-Peralta por su contribución editorial a la versión en español de este libro y por asegurarse que mis palabras y sentimientos pudieran trascender culturas y lenguaje.

To the Children of the World...

...especially to my Grandchildren

Para los Niños del Mundo...

...y en especial para mis Nietos

DEDICATION

This book was originally inspired by my first granddaughter, Shelby Faith Ledward. When she was born, almost 20 years ago, my world opened up to a whole new level of awareness, thankfulness, protectiveness, and continuity. I felt a deeper sense of responsibility to make the world a better place for this beautiful new being. I remember seeing her for the first time and knowing that she was my granddaughter and that I would see her through life—that she was a part of me—and that I would always be a part of her.

I distinctly remember one of our first outings with Shelby. My husband Bill and I took our granddaughter to a gathering at a friend's house and introduced her to everyone. I was so proud of my new role as grandmother and aware of the precious gift that my granddaughter was to me. So as Bill and I went around the room introducing her as Shelby Faith something special happened. When we introduced Shelby to a young woman, whom I did not know, she said, "Oh, Shelby Faith—like "Shall be Faith on Earth." It was in that moment that I knew there really was a much deeper purpose to the little person I was holding.

I wrote this book when Shelby was a toddler because I was inspired by the concept of "Shall be Faith on Earth." My dream was that this book be fun and interactive, and that it would somehow bring families closer together. It seemed like writing this book would contribute to my granddaughter's life, the lives of my future grandchildren, and perhaps the lives of other children and their families. This book sat in my desk drawer for many years. I am not sure why. I would often take it out and look at it and put it back. Now, living in an age of computers, e-books, iPhones and such, the book brings a whole new meaning to the word "interactive." I hope that families will find this book interactive—whether it is used as an old-fashioned lap book or a new-fangled e-book.

I now have two other amazing grandchildren, Isabella and Sean. I say it is time to get this book out of the desk drawer and share with others because now, more than ever, it seems like we need to be reminded that there "Shall be Faith on Earth."

DEDICATORIA

Este libro fué originalmente inspirado por mi primera nieta, Shelby Faith Ledward. Cuando ella nació, ya hace 20 años, mi mundo se abrió a un nuevo nivel de consciencia, agradecimiento, cuidado (atención) y persistencia. Sentí una profunda responsabilidad para hacer que este mundo fuera un mejor lugar para este hermoso nuevo ser. Recuerdo verla por primera vez y saber que era mi nieta y que yo la vería a través de la vida – que ella era parte de mí – y que siempre yo sería parte de ella.

Claramente recuerdo una de nuestras primeras salidas con Shelby. Mi esposo, Bill y yo llevamos a nuestra nieta a una reunión a la casa de un amigo y se la presentamos a todos. Yo estaba tan orgullosa en mi nuevo papel de abuela y consciente del regalo precioso que mi nieta era para mí. Entonces, mientras Bill y yo recorríamos el cuarto presentándola como Shelby Faith, algo especial aconteció. Cuando le presentamos a Shelby a una mujer joven a quien yo no conocía, ella nos dijo: 'Oh, Shelby Faith – como 'Habrá Fe en la Tierra.' En ese momento supe que de verdad había un propósito mucho más profundo para la existencia de esta pequeña persona que tenía en mis brazos.

Escribí este libro cuando Shelby era ya una niña pequeña, inspirada por el concepto de "Habra Fé en la Tierra" Mi sueño era que este libro fuera interactivo y divertido y que de alguna manera acercara a las familias. Parecería que al escribir este libro yo contribuiría a la vida de mi nieta, a la vida de mis futuros nietos y tal vez a la vida de otros niños y sus familias. Sin embargo, este libro quedó guardado en un cajón de mi escritorio por muchos años, no estoy segura por qué. A menudo lo sacaba y lo miraba y lo volvía a guardar. Ahora, viviendo en la era de las computadoras, libros electrónicos, teléfonos celulares y demás, el libro le da un nuevo significado a la palabra 'interactivo.' Espero que las familias encuentren este libro participativo ya sea que lo usen como una lectura tradicional o un libro electrónico dinámico. Actualmente tengo otros dos nietos maravillosos, Isabela y Sean. Así es que es hora de sacar este libro del cajón del escritorio y compartirlo con otras personas. Ahora más que nunca me parece que necesitamos recordar que habrá 'Fe en la Tierra.'

Dear Parents & Kids

This book is for every kind of family willing to sit down and share thoughts and feelings and ideas. It is for your family. It's a book for reading, talking about, and doing. It's a book designed to help you bring a deeper love to each other and a better understanding of one another. It's about listening and hearing one another. It's also about healing one another. It will be a special experience for everyone.

Remember: there is no right or wrong way of doing the readings and activities in this book. It's all about learning to have more fun together as a family. Feel free to write in this book, color the pictures, and add your family photos. Use your imagination and have fun! Here are some suggested materials to use if you are reading a hard copy of this book: crayons, felt pens, colored pencils, stamp pad and ink.

P.S.

Parents, because this book is designed for children of all ages, the text and/or concepts, in some cases, may be too sophisticated for your child/children to understand. Please take the "seed" of the thought and put it into words your child/children can understand.

ENJOY!!!

Queridos Padres y Niños

Este libro es para todo tipo de familias, dispuestas a sentarse a compartir sus sentimientos e ideas. Es para tu familia. Este es un libro para leerlo, discutirlo y trabajarlo. Este es un libro diseñado para ayudar a la las familias a compartir su amor a un nivel más profundo y para ayudar a entenderse mejor los unos a los otros. Se trata de aprender a oírse y escucharse los unos a los otros. También se trata de como aprender a sanarse el uno al otro. Esta será una experiencia muy especial para todos.

Recuerden: no existe una manera única para realizar las lecturas y llevar a cabo las actividades de este libro. Se trata de aprender a divertirse más juntos, como familia. Siéntanse con la libertad de escribir en este libro, de iluminar los dibujos y de añadir fotos de la familia. ¡Usen su imaginación y diviértanse!

Aquí les sugerimos algunos materiales que pueden utilizar si están leyendo una copia de este libro: crayones, plumas, lápices de color, sellos y tinta.

P.S. Padres de familia, ya que este libro está diseñado para niños de todas las edades, el texto y/o los conceptos, en algunos casos, pueden ser un poco sofisticados para que su/s niño/niños los comprenda/n. Por Favor tomen la 'semilla' de la idea y traten de explicarla con palabras que su/s niño/ niños pueden comprender mejor.

¡DISFRUTEN!

PARENT SMART

"The More You Know, the More You Grow."
Quote by Luther H. Stuckey

It has often been said that kids don't come with an instruction manual. It's true—most of our parenting "skills" have been handed down from generation to generation. So parents wind up doing what their parents did to them—even though they might have vowed never to be like their parent. Then one day, you hear yourself say to one of your offspring something like, "Close the door behind you" and it is in that moment that you realize you have become your parent. Well, for some of us, that's motivation enough to want to do something way different.

The good news is that parents/caregivers seem to want to know more and more about their role. We are even willing to take parenting classes, read books on parenting, and join parent groups. This can be really empowering. I have taught parenting classes for over 30 years and I have seen many common themes once parents open up to talk:

• Parents are relieved to hear that they were not alone—that many other parents are experiencing the same things

• Parents become a resource and support for one another

• Parents just need a way to talk things out about what is going on with their kid

• Parents want to be better parents—no matter what

With that in mind, I would like to

PADRE INGENIOSO

'Mientras Más se Sabe, Más Se Crece'
Cita de Luther H. Stuckey

Se ha dicho que los niños no vienen al mundo con un manual de instrucciones. Es cierto – la mayoría de los 'conocimientos' de ser padres se van pasado de generación en generación. Por lo que los padres terminan haciendo lo que sus padres les hacían a ellos – aunque alguna vez juramos 'nunca ser como mi madre.' un día, escuchamos decirle a uno de nuestros hijos algo así como 'Cierra la puerta al salir' y es en ese momento nos damos cuenta de que nos hemos convertido en nuestra madre.

Bueno, para algunos de nosotros, ésta es motivación suficiente para querer hacer cambios importantes.

Lo bueno es que tanto los padres de familia/como los guardianes quieren aprender cómo llevar a cabo su papel. Algunos hasta estamos dispuestos a tomar clases de cómo ser mejores padres, leemos libros, y nos unimos a grupos de padres de familia. Esto de verdad puede ser enaltecedor. Recuerdo hace unos 30 años haber dado clases a padres de familia y observar muchos temas en común:

• Los padres de familia se tranquilizan al escuchar que no están solos – que hay otros padres que están viviendo las mismas cosas

• Los padres de familia llegan a ser un recurso de apoyo entre ellos mismos

• Los padres de familia tan sólo necesitan hablar sobre las cosas que están viviendo con su niño(a)

offer some ideas on how to use this book as a learning tool for you and your child. Because you really are your child's first teacher, you get to impart knowledge and values to your children. So not only will you be teaching the "ABCs," you will also be teaching things like responsibility, trustworthiness, honesty, and teamwork. This book is the vehicle for imparting both kinds of experiences—knowledge through discovery and discussion and hands-on activities that are designed to be fun and educational at the same time.

There is an important trade secret I would like to share. Some of us in the field of education call it "the teachable moment." It is a moment in time when you realize that you have an opportunity to teach or reinforce a concept to your child. So for instance, if you are driving in your car and you come up to a STOP sign, you have all kinds of opportunities to talk with your child to expand his or her learning.

Depending on the age of the child, some of the following questions or comments are examples:

• What color is the sign?
• What are the letters on the sign?
• What word does it spell?
• What shape is the sign?
• Why do we have to take turns stopping?

• Los padres siempre quieren ser mejores padres

Tomando esto en cuenta, me gustaría ofrecerles algunas ideas de cómo hacer uso de este libro como una herramienta de aprendizaje tanto para usted como para su niño. En realidad, es usted el primer maestro de su niño, y por ello le toca darles sabiduría y valores a sus niños. No sólo se trata de enseñarles el 'ABC,' sino también enseñarles otros valores como responsabilidad, confianza, honradez, honestidad y trabajo en equipo. Este libro es un vehículo para impartir ambos tipos de experiencias – conocimiento a través del descubrimiento y debate, y actividades manuales que están diseñadas para ser tanto divertidas pero también educativas.

Les voy a revelar un secreto que sabemos los que trabajamos en el campo de la educación. Tenemos algo que se llama 'momento de aprendizaje.' Este es un momento en el que nos damos cuenta que existe una buena oportunidad para enseñarle o reforzarle un concepto a nuestro hijo. Por ejemplo si se encuentra manejando en su carro y llega a una señal de ALTO, tiene todo tipo de oportunidades para hablar con su hijo y ampliar sus conocimientos.

Un ejemplo sería (dependiendo de la edad del niño) hacer una de las siguientes preguntas o comentarios:

• ¿De qué color es la señal?
• ¿Cuáles son las letras de la señal?

(Continued on next page)

(Continúa en la siguiente página)

Here are some ways to have "teachable moments" while using *My Family Matters To Me*. besides reading the text/story on the left hand side of the book, you can discuss:

The illustration—Ask what the picture means to them? What things are in the picture? A good time to discuss "Remember when..."

The letters and the word—Ask about the letters that make up the word. Do they know any other words that begin with that letter?

On the right side of the book where most of the text is, "teachable moments" would include:

What letter is at the top?—capital and lower case versions of the same letter

What is the word at the top of the page? What are the letters in that word?

Read the text and find the bold print word in the text.

Find the variation of the word in the text—sometimes it has an "ing" on the end, but the "root" word is the same.

Do the activity together and ask your child to tell you about it.

Just listen—someone to listen to them is what all kids really want.

• ¿Qué palabra puedes deletrear?
• ¿Qué forma tiene la señal?
• ¿Por qué debemos tomar turnos para parar frente a la señal?

Aquí mostramos algunas maneras de iniciar 'momentos de aprendizaje' mientras usan el libro *Mi Familia Me Importa*. Además de leer el texto/narración también pueden discutir lo siguiente:

Los dibujos – pregunte qué significan los dibujos para ellos. ¿Qué cosas hay en el dibujo? Un buen momento para conversar 'Recuerdas cuando...'

Las palabras y sus letras – pregunte cuales son las letras que componen la palabra.

¿Conocen otras palabras que comiencen con la misma letra?

Otros "momentos de aprendizaje" pueden ser:

¿Qué letra está al inicio de la página? ¿Cómo es la mayúscula y la minúscula de la misma letra?

¿Cuál es la palabra al inicio de la página?

¿Qué letras que componen esa palabra?

Lee el texto y encuentra la palabra en negrita. Encuentra la misma palabra en el texto – pero con otra conjugación, a veces tiene otra terminación, pero la "raíz es la misma. Hagan las actividades juntos y pregunte a su niño que le digan algo sobre esta actividad.

Simplemente escuche lo que el niño platique – todos los niños quieren que los escuchen.

Introduction...Family

The word **family** means a lot of different things to different people. It's a word that usually brings up lots of feelings for everyone. It's as though everyone belongs to some kind of family. The traditional family used to be a mom, dad, and kids (usually two kids, ideally a boy and a girl, in that order).

Today, we see that families can come in all different ways. Here are some examples:

- A mom with a kid (s)
- A dad with a kid (s)
- Grandparents with a kid (s)
- Two moms with a kid (s)
- Two dads with a kid (s)
- An aunt/uncle with a kid (s)
- A blended family with a stepparent and sometimes stepsisters and brothers
- A foster family with foster children

(Continued on next page)

Introducción...Familia

La palabra **familia** puede significar muchas cosas para diferentes personas. Es una palabra que normalmente produce muchos sentimientos a todos. Es porque todos pertenecemos a algún tipo de familia. La familia tradicional era la mamá, el papá e hijos (usualmente dos niños, idealmente un niño y una niña, en esa orden).

Hoy en día, vemos que las familias son muy diferentes. Aquí hay algunos ejemplos:

- Una Mamá con hijo(s)
- Un Papá con hijo(s)
- Los Abuelos con los niño(s)
- Dos mamás con hijo(s)
- Dos papás con hijo(s)
- Un Tía/tío con niños(s)
- Una familia combinada con padrastro/madrastra y a veces hermanastros y hermanos
- Niños adoptados con su familia adoptiva

(Continúa en la siguiente página)

- A family with adopted kids
- A team, troop, squad or platoon

Sometimes family can be a family of friends, a church family, or a retirement family. Sometimes even strangers can feel "like family." There's even a "universal family," meaning everyone in the whole world is connected in some way because we are all living here on earth together at this time. Family is about being in relationship with one another, and can happen anywhere, anytime.

Families can share these things: being connected to one another, important values, unconditional love, and respect for one another. Families can provide a "You can do it" attitude and inspiration through mutual communication. Families can be fun. They can also—very importantly—provide a spiritual foundation for life.

This book is dedicated to helping families share more good times together. This book is to be read together; it is a book to read with your children rather than to your children. It's an interactive book designed to promote communication and discovery about who each person is. It's a book for reading, doing, and listening. It's a book for listening to one another. It's a book for loving and learning.

LET'S START THE JOURNEY...

• Un equipo, un grupo, una tropa o pelotón

A veces la familia puede ser una familia de amigos, una familia de la iglesia o una familia de jubilados. A veces hasta extraños pueden sentirse 'como si fueran familia.' También existe la 'familia universal' que incluye a todos los seres que vivimos juntos aquí en la tierra ya que de alguna manera estamos conectados. Una familia significa estar relacionados unos con otros y puede darse en cualquier lugar y a cualquier hora.

Las familias pueden compartir lo siguiente: una conexión del uno con el otro, valores personales, amor incondicional y respeto del uno con el otro. Las familias pueden proporcionar una actitud positiva de 'Poder lograrlo todo' y pueden inspirar a través de una comunicación mutua. Las familias pueden ser divertidas. También pueden—de manera muy importante—proporcionar una fundación espiritual para toda la vida.

Este libro está dedicado a ayudar a las familias a compartir muchos más momentos positivos juntos. Este libro es para leerlo juntos; es un libro para leerlo con sus niños y no a sus niños. Es un libro interactivo diseñado para promover comunicación y descubrimiento sobre quienes somos cada uno de nosotros. Es un libro para leerlo, trabajarlo y escucharlo. Es un libro que nos ayudara a escucharnos el uno al otro. Es un libro para infundir amor y aprendizaje.

COMENCEMOS LA JORNADA...

WHO IS IN YOUR FAMILY?

Draw a picture of your family.

Add photos if you like.

¿QUIÉN ES PARTE DE TU FAMILIA?

Haz un dibujo de tu familia.

Añade fotos si lo deseas.

WHAT DO YOU LOVE ABOUT YOUR FAMILY?

xoxoxoxoxoxoxoxoxoxoxoxoxoxoxoxoxoxoxoxoxoxoxox

¿QUÉ ES LO QUE MAS TE GUSTA DE TU FAMILIA?

xoxoxoxoxoxoxoxoxoxoxoxoxoxoxoxoxoxoxoxoxoxoxox

AWARENESS

(CONCIENCIA)

Sound
(Sonido)

Touch
(Tocar)

Taste
(Sabor)

Smell
(Oler)

Sight
(Ver)

AA   AWARENESS

Awareness is an awesome word. The dictionary says **awareness** is being "informed, conscious, alive and awake." That means being present—alive and aware—right now. For instance, check your own **awareness** level. Look around you. What do you see? Look for color, size, and texture. What do you smell? What odors are in the air? Is there a taste on your tongue? What sounds do you hear? What can you touch? Keep sharing your **awareness** with someone you know. Our **awareness** tells us we are alive and makes us aware of who we are.

Make a drawing of you and write or tell about your **awareness**.

- I see...

- I smell...

- I taste...

- I hear...

- I touch...

- I am...(Write your name)

AA   CONCIENCIA

La **conciencia** es una palabra maravillosa. El diccionario dice que la **conciencia** es estar "informado(a), consciente, vivo(a) y despierto(a)." Eso significa estar presente, vivo(a) y consciente ahorita. Por ejemplo, verifica el nivel de tu **conciencia**. Mira a tu alrededor. ¿Qué ves? Busca el tamaño, el color y la textura. ¿Qué hueles? ¿Qué olores hay en el aire? ¿Hay un sabor en tu boca? ¿Qué sonidos escuchas? ¿Qué puedes tocar? Sigue compartiendo este reconocimiento con alguien que conozcas. Nuestra **conciencia** nos dice que estamos vivos y nos hace conscientes de quienes somos.

Dibújate a ti mismo y escribe o habla con alguien sobre tu **conciencia**.

- Veo...

- Huelo...

- Pruebo...

- Escucho...

- Toco...

- Yo soy... (Escribe tu nombre)

Belly Breathing

(Respiración de vientre)

BB BELLY BREATHING

Belly Breathing helps each of us become a better person. **Belly Breathing** slows us down. When we slow down our body, it allows us to slow down and quiet our mind. This is when our Spirit can also be quieted. **Belly Breathing** is especially good when we are feeling stressed or upset.

Here's how you can do **Belly Breathing**:

1. Find a quiet place, and sit or lie down comfortably.

2. Take a full deep breath through your nose and imagine that your breath is coming from the bottom of your belly. You might even want to slowly count to yourself as you are doing this: 1—2—3—4. If you rest your hand on your belly as you're doing this, your hand will naturally move away from your **belly**.

- You will also notice that your chest expands as you do this.
- Some people like to hold their breath for one count.
- Gently release your breath through slightly parted lips.
- Repeat, and enjoy relaxation.

Some people do **Belly Breathing** by pretending to blow out a candle. Some people imagine exhaling or breathing out the things that stress them. Take a few minutes and practice **Belly Breathing**. How do you feel after **Belly Breathing**?

I feel...

BB RESPIRACIÓN DE VIENTRE

La Respiración de Vientre nos ayuda a ser mejores personas. **Respirar con el Vientre** nos permite tranquilizarnos. Cuando nos movemos más lento, esto nos permite calmar y descansar nuestra mente. Esto es cuando nuestra Espíritu puede tranquilizarse. **La Respiración de Vientre** es buena cuando nos sentimos tensos o enojados.

Aquí explicamos cómo hacer **La Respiración de Vientre**:

1. Encuentra un lugar tranquilo, y siéntate o acuéstese cómodamente.

2. Respira profundamente por la nariz e imagina que tu respiración viene del fondo de tu vientre. Si quieres puedes contar con la mente: 1-2-3-4... mientras respiras. Si pones tu mano en tu vientre mientras haces esto, vas a ver que tu mano se mueve al ritmo de tu **vientre**.

- También notarás que tu pecho crece mientras respiras.
- Algunas personas aguantan la respiración mientras cuentan.
- Separa tus labios y deja salir poco a poco el aire por la boca.
- Repite este ejercicio y relájate.

Algunas personas hacen la **Respiración de Vientre** pretendiendo que van a apagar una vela. Algunas personas imaginan que sacan las cosas que los tensionan mediante esta respiración. Practica la **Respiración de Vientre** durante unos minutos. ¿Cómo te sientes después de hacer La **Respiración de Vientre**?   Me siento...

Cc COMMUNICATION

There are lots of ways to communicate. Babies communicate by crying. People can also communicate without words by using facial expressions or their hands for sign language. Much **communication** is not done with words. It's nonverbal. The ways we stand or sit, or the "looks" we give one another are examples of nonverbal **communication**.

Communication involves a real desire to listen and to be heard. Some **communication** words and styles block real **communication**. Some roadblock words are "but" or "however." These words erase positive words that come before them.

Using "and" helps separate the person from his or her behavior. It still gives unconditional love, even though you might be upset with the person. An example is, "I love you, but..." Remember: "butt out" of but, and use "and" instead. It would sound like this, "I love you, and..." It has a whole different feeling to it.

Using this style of **communication** can help us resolve conflicts because it is friendlier.

Now you give someone an "and" sentence. An example: "I like being your friend and sometimes..."

Cc COMUNICACIÓN

Hay un montón de maneras de comunicarse. Los bebés se comunican llorando. Las personas también pueden comunicarse sin palabras mediante el uso de las expresiones faciales o con las manos mediante el lenguaje a señas. Mucha **comunicación** no se hace con palabras. Esta es la **comunicación** no verbal. La forma en la que nos paramos o nos sentamos, o la forma en la que nos miramos son ejemplos de una comunicación no verbal.

La **comunicación** implica un verdadero deseo de escuchar y de ser escuchado. Algunas palabras y estilos de **comunicación** bloquean la **comunicación** autentica. Algunas palabras evasivas son "pero" o "sin embargo". Estas palabras eliminan nuestras palabras positivas. Usar palabras como "y" ayuda a diferenciar a la persona de su comportamiento. Y nos transmite una sensación de amor aunque no nos guste lo que la persona nos dice. Un ejemplo es: "Te amo, pero..." Recuerda utilizar la palabra y en lugar de pero. El ejemplo anterior sonaría: "Te amo y..." Tiene un sentimiento completamente diferente.

Usar este estilo de **comunicación** nos puede ayudar a resolver conflictos, ya que es más amigable.

Escribe un ejemplo usando la palabra "y". Un ejemplo seria, "Me gusta ser tu amigo(a) y a veces..."

Dinosaur thinking

(PENSAMIENTO DE DINOSAURIO)

Dᴅ Dɪɴᴏsᴀᴜʀ-Tʜɪɴᴋɪɴɢ

Dinosaur-thinking: what does that mean? In this book, it means thinking that is "Jurassic", or stuck in the past. It means thinking how you should be or ought to be. Typically, **dinosaur-thinking** limits our ability to forgive ourselves for our mistakes, and makes us think we should be perfect. So when we aren't perfect, it makes us feel bad. It also limits our perception of others so that we don't see things from another person's point of view. Here are some examples of **dinosaur-thinking**:

- "Be perfect."
- "It has to be my way."
- "I know I'm right all the time."
- "I am never right."
- "I am stupid."

Can you think of some examples of your **dinosaur-thinking**?

Dᴅ Pᴇɴsᴀᴍɪᴇɴᴛᴏ ᴅᴇ Dɪɴᴏsᴀᴜʀɪᴏ

Pensamiento de dinosaurio: ¿Qué significa eso? En este libro, significa pensar que en el "Jurásico" o atorado en el pasado. Significa pensar cómo algo debe o debería de ser. Por lo general, el **pensamiento de dinosaurio** limita nuestra capacidad de perdonarnos a nosotros mismos por errores que cometimos, y nos hace pensar que deberíamos ser perfectos. Así que cuando no somos perfectos esto nos hace sentir mal. También limita nuestra percepción de los demás y no nos deja ver las cosas desde el punto de vista de otras personas. Aquí hay algunos ejemplos del **pensamiento de dinosaurio**:

- "Sé perfecto."
- "Tiene que ser a mi manera."
- "Sé que siempre tengo la razón."
- "Nunca tengo la razón."
- "Soy un estúpido."

¿Puedes pensar en algunos ejemplos en donde tienes **pensamiento de dinosaurio**?

EXCEL
(SOBRESALIR)

Ee   Excel

When you **excel** in something, it means doing the very best you can. How do you know if you **excel** in something? You feel energized and excited! When we feel energized and excited about something, our body actually releases our own body chemicals called endorphins. Endorphins help us feel excellent!

What are some things that you **excel** in?

Are you a terrific speller? Can you create wonderful pictures? Are you a whiz at math? Can you play a musical instrument?

Is there something you would like to **excel** in? What would that be? How would you go about doing it?

Ee   Sobresalir

Cuando **sobresales** en algo, significa hacer algo lo mejor que puedas. ¿Cómo sabes si **sobresales** en algo? ¡Te sientes contento y emocionado! Cuando nos sentimos con energía y emoción por algo, nuestro cuerpo libera unos químicos llamados endorfinas.

¡Las endorfinas nos ayudan a sentirnos excelentes!

¿Cuáles son algunas cosas en las que tú **sobresales?**

¿Sabes deletrear muy bien? ¿Puedes crear dibujos maravillosos? ¿Eres un genio para las matemáticas? ¿Puedes tocar un instrumento musical?

¿Hay algo en lo que te gustaría **sobresalir**? ¿Que sería esto? ¿Cómo lo podrías lograr?

FAITH

(Fe)

Ff Faith

There shall be Shelby **Faith** on Earth—There shall be **FAITH** On Earth

Faith is:
- having courage
- believing that things happen for a reason even though we don't understand why
- having positive thoughts
- practicing good deeds
- having a purpose to the things we do
- believing in something greater than ourselves

What does **faith** mean to you?

Has there been a time when something seemed impossible, yet you were still able to do it?

That's an example of **faith**! Write about it here!

Ff Fe

Habrá Shelby **Faith** en la tierra-Habrá **FE** en la tierra.

La **fe** es:
- tener valor
- creer que las cosas suceden por alguna razón, aunque no entendamos por qué
- tener pensamientos positivos
- hacer buenas acciones
- hacer las cosas con un propósito
- creer en algo más grande que nosotros mismos

¿Qué significa la **fe** para ti?

¿Alguna vez hiciste algo que parecía imposible, aun así fuiste capaz de hacerlo?

¡Eso es un ejemplo de la **fe**! ¡Escribe aquí tu experiencia!

GROW

(CRECER)

Gg Grow

Human beings need many things in order to **grow**. We need healthy food, clothing, shelter, and lots of love for us to **grow**. There is another kind of growing that we do. That kind of growing happens when we take on new challenges or experiences, and learn from them. That kind of growing gives us confidence. We need confidence in order to try new things, like riding a bike or climbing a mountain.

Find a picture of yourself as a baby, and you now. Put them here. List all the ways you have grown.

Gg Crecer

Los humanos necesitan muchas cosas para **crecer**. Necesitamos alimentación sana, ropa, vivienda y mucho amor para que podamos **crecer**. Sin embargo, tenemos otro tipo de crecimiento Ese tipo de crecimiento ocurre cuando asumimos nuevos retos y experiencias y aprendemos cuando los llevamos a cabo. Ese tipo de crecimiento nos da seguridad y confianza. Necesitamos confianza para intentar cosas nuevas, como andar en bicicleta o escalar una montaña.

Busca una foto de ti cuando eras bebé y una de ahora. Pégalas aquí. Haz una lista de todas las formas en las que haz crecido.

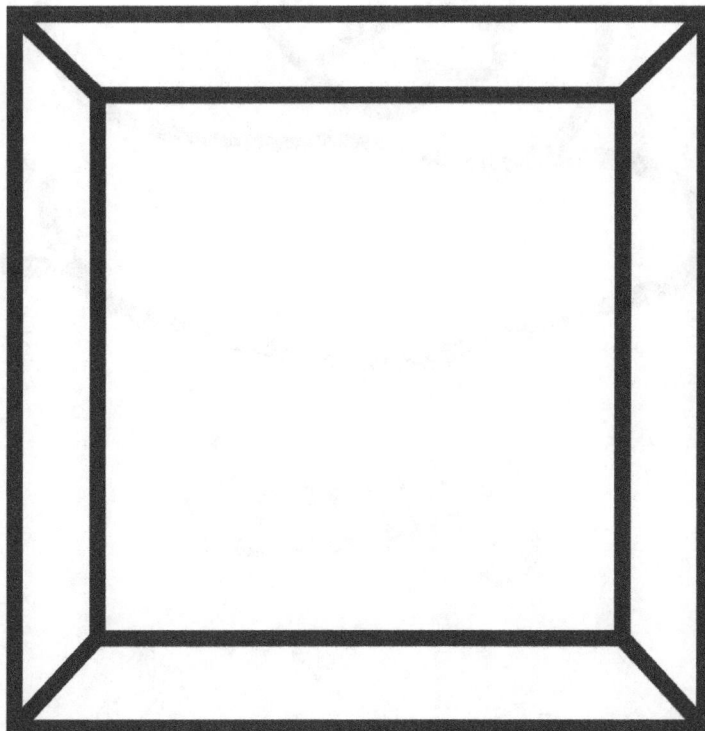

HH   HANDS

Helping **hands** bring honor, pride, and harmony to the things you do. **Hands** are for healing. **Hands** are for creating. Trace your hand here and fill in the things you do with your **hands**! **Hands** are for:

- Holding another person's hand
- Brushing your teeth
- Petting a dog or cat
- Growing a garden
- Gathering flowers
- Painting a picture
- Playing with toys
- Setting the table
- Creating music
- Tying knots
- Cooking
- Praying

HH   MANOS

Unas **manos** que ayudan le brindan honor, orgullo y armonía a las cosas que hacemos. Las **manos** son para curar. Las **manos** son para crear. ¡Traza tu mano aquí y escribe en ella las cosas que haces con tus **manos**! Las **manos** son para:

- Tomar la mano de otra persona
- Cepillarse los dientes
- Acariciar a un gato o a un perro
- Cultivar un jardín
- Recoger flores
- Pintar un cuadro
- Jugar con tus juguetes
- Poner la mesa
- Crear música
- Hacer nudos
- Cocinar
- Rezar

IMAGINATION

(IMAGINACIÓN)

ⅠⅠ IMAGINATION

Imagination starts with "I"

I create...

I dream of...

I invent...

I see...

I imagine...

I write...

I draw...

I dance...

I read...

You have a BIG **imagination**. How do you use your **imagination**? Tell someone about something you imagine! Or, draw something you imagine.

ⅠⅠ IMAGINACIÓN

La **imaginación** comienza "conmigo"

Yo creo...

Yo sueño con...

Yo invento...

Yo veo...

Imagino que...

Yo escribo...

Yo Dibujo...

Yo bailo...

Yo leo...

Tú tienes una GRAN **imaginación** ¿Cómo utilizas tu **imaginación**? ¡Comparte con alguien algo que imaginas! Imagina algo y dibújalo.

JOURNEY

(JORNADA)

JJ   JOURNEY

A long time ago, someone said life was like a **journey**. Life has many ups and downs just like a roller coaster. Sometimes we feel "up" or happy when good things happen to us. Sometimes we feel "down" or sad when things don't turn out the way we want them to.

Do you sometimes feel "up" or "down?"

Write or tell about the times when you feel up:

Write or tell about the times when you feel down:

Draw a picture to show your feelings.

JJ   JORNADA

Hace mucho tiempo, alguien dijo que la vida era como una **jornada**. La vida tiene muchos altos y bajos al igual que una montaña rusa. A veces estamos "arriba" y felices cuando nos suceden cosas buenas. A veces, estamos "abajo" o tristes cuando las cosas no salen como queremos.

¿A veces te sientes "arriba" o "abajo"?

Escribe o platica con alguien de las veces en las que te has sentido arriba.

Escribe o platica con alguien de las veces en las que te has sentido abajo.

Haz un dibujo que demuestre tus sentimientos.

KNOWLEDGE

(CONOCIMIENTO)

MATH

READING

(MATEMÁTICAS)   (LECTURA)

Este Certificado Es Para:

_____

Por Ser Bueno En:

_____

Kk KNOWLEDGE

Knowledge includes knowing what you know, and understanding what you know. **Knowledge** comes from learning and experiencing. Sometimes **knowledge** comes from books, and sometimes it come from living life.

Remember, learning is the key to **knowledge**.

Someone once said, "It's not <u>how</u> smart you are, its <u>how</u> you are smart." Keep learning from books and learning from life.

So <u>how</u> are you smart? Put a check mark next to the ones that describe you:

____ I make friends easily.
____ I understand myself and help others.
____ I have physical and athletic abilities.
____ I am good at math.
____ I am good at music.
____ I am good at science.
____ I am good at writing stories.
____ I can easily put things together.
____ Other things I'm good at:

Kk CONOCIMIENTO

El **conocimiento** incluye saber lo que conoces y comprender lo que conoces. El **conocimiento** se genera del aprendizaje y la experiencia. A veces el **conocimiento** viene de los libros y a veces viene de la vida.

Recuerda, el **conocimiento** es la clave para aprender.

Alguien dijo alguna vez, "no es que tan inteligente eres, sino como eres inteligente." Sigue aprendiendo de los libros y de la vida.

De qué manera eres inteligente? Pon una marca junto a las maneras que te describen a ti:

____ Puedo hacer amigos fácilmente.
____ Me conozco bien y trato de ayudar a los demás
____ Tengo habilidades físicas y atléticas.
____ Soy bueno para las matemáticas.
____ Soy bueno en la música.
____ Soy bueno en la ciencia.
____ Soy bueno para escribir historias.
____ Puedo armar cosas fácilmente.
____ Otras cosas en las que soy bueno....

This Certificate Is Presented to:

_____

For Being Good At:

_____

LOVE

(AMOR)

LL LOVE

The greatest "L" word of all is **love**. **Love** makes all good things happen. **Love** makes our world go around.

How does it feel when you **love** someone? How does someone make you feel when they **love** you? Tell or write about that here.

Tell or write the name of someone you **love**.

Who else do you love in your life? Draw or put a picture here of that person.

Is there something else you **love**? A dog? A cat?

Tell or write the name of something else you **love**.

LL AMOR

Amor es una palabra grandiosa. El **amor** hace que todas las cosas buenas sucedan. El **amor** hace que nuestro mundo gire.

¿Cómo te sientes cuando **amas** a alguien? ¿Cómo te sientes cuando alguien te **ama**? Platícalo con alguien o escríbelo aquí.

Platica o escribe el nombre de alguien a quien tú **amas**.

¿A qué otra persona **amas** en tu vida? Dibuja o pega aquí la foto de esa persona

¿Hay algo más que **amas**? ¿Un perro? ¿Un gato?

Platica o escribe el nombre de algo más que **ames**.

I LOVE _____.   Yo AMO _____ ▫

Miracle

(Milagro)

MM MIRACLE

Ask for a **miracle** and see what happens! Sometimes miracles are small, such as finding a parking place up front at a busy mall (that's a grown-up's **miracle**), or finding a shiny penny, or finding a white feather, or finding a special friend. Sometimes miracles start off little and grow big, like you!

Draw a picture of yourself when you were very little.

Draw a picture of yourself now.

Remember—YOU are a **MIRACLE**!

MM MILAGRO

¡Pide un **milagro** y observa que pasa! A veces los milagros son pequeños, como encontrar un lugar de estacionamiento frente a un centro comercial (éste es un **milagro** para adultos), o encontrar una moneda en el suelo, o encontrar una pluma de pájaro blanca, o encontrar un amigo especial. A veces los milagros comienzan siendo pequeños pero poco a poco van creciendo, ¡al igual que tú!

Haz un dibujo de ti mismo cuando eras muy pequeñito.

Haz un dibujo actual de ti mismo. Recuerda que—¡TÚ eres un **milagro**!

NURTURE

(NUTRIR)

NN NURTURE

To "**nurture**" means to take care of or to feed. How do you feed your body ("body" food)? How do you feed your mind ("brain" food)? How do you feed your soul/spirit ("soul"/spirit food)? Who are the people that help **nurture** you? Are there special places, things, or pets that help **nurture** you?

Here's a beginning list:

<u>I take care of my Body</u>
I eat fruit

<u>I take care of my Mind</u>
I read

<u>I take care of my Soul/Spirit</u>
I spend time with friends

See if you can come up with at least 5 more ways to **nurture** yourself everyday with special people, places, and things.

NN NUTRIR

Nutrir significa cuidar o alimentar a alguien o algo. ¿Cómo alimentas tu cuerpo (alimento del cuerpo)? ¿Cómo alimentas tu mente (alimento de mente)? ¿Cómo alimentas tu alma/espíritu (alimento del alma/espíritu)? ¿Quiénes son las personas que ayudan a **nutrirte**? ¿Hay lugares especiales, cosas, o animales que ayudan a nutrirte?

Aquí tienes una lista para comenzar:

<u>Alimento a mi cuerpo</u>
Como fruta

<u>Alimento a mi mente</u>
Leo

<u>Alimento a mi alma/espíritu</u>
Paso tiempo con mis amigos

Ve si puedes agregar por lo menos 5 maneras más en las que te nutres todos los días, con cosas, lugares, o personas.

Open

(ABIERTO)

Oo Open

Sometimes being **open** means being willing to have a new idea about something or someone. We can be **open** to trying new foods, making new friends, and learning new things like riding a bike. When we are **open** to new ideas, it helps us think about things in a different way.

Sometimes we can be **open** when someone wants to apologize for saying or doing mean things. If that happens, we can make a decision to be **open** and forgive them, or heal our hurt. (S. Austin)

Are you willing to be **open** or try something new? What would that be?

Circle the new things that you would be open to.

I would be **open** to...
- Trying a new food
- Learning a musical instrument
- Learning a new dance
- Going down the tallest slide
- Learning to ride a bike
- Learning to do math
- Forgiving a friend
- Skydiving
- Waterskiing
- Making new friends
- Learning a new language
- Skateboarding

Oo Abierto

A veces ser **abierto** significa que estamos dispuestos a tener nuevas ideas acerca de algo o de alguien. Podemos ser **abiertos** cuando probamos nuevas comidas, hacemos nuevos amigos y aprendemos cosas nuevas como andar en bicicleta. Cuando estamos **abiertos** a nuevas ideas, esto nos ayuda a pensar de una manera diferente.

Podemos ser **abiertos** cuando alguien quiere disculparse con nosotros por haber dicho o hecho algo malo. Si eso sucede, podemos tomar la decisión de ser **abiertos** y aceptar su disculpa para así poder sanar nuestra herida. (S. Austin)

¿Estás dispuesto a ser **abierto** o a intentar algo nuevo? ¿Qué seria esto?

Encierra en un círculo las cosas a las que estás dispuesto a ser **abierto**.

Yo estoy **abierto** a...
- Intentar una nueva comida
- Aprender a tocar un instrumento musical
- Aprender un nuevo baile
- Bajar por el tobogán más alto
- Aprender a andar en bicicleta
- Aprender matemáticas
- Disculpar a un amigo
- Hacer paracaidismo
- Esquiar en el agua
- Hacer nuevos amigos
- Aprender un nuevo idioma
- Andar en patín/patineta

POSITIVE

(POSITIVO)

Pp Positive

Staying **positive** in what sometimes seems like a not-so-**positive** world is hard to do. Keep focusing on **positive** people and experiences. See the good in others.

Positive attitudes give you a **positive** perspective in life. It's like the story about the elevator operator who was humming and singing early one Monday morning. One passenger seemed particularly irritated by the man's mood and snapped, "What are you so happy about?" "Well, sir," replied the man happily, "I've never lived this day before!" (Adapted from the story by John Maxwell, *The Winning Attitude*, p.43)

What kinds of things do you feel **positive** about?

Suppose it was a rainy day and you could not go out to play. How would you make it a **positive** day?

Pp Positivo

Mantenerse **positivo** en un mundo que a veces parece no ser tan positivo, es algo difícil. Continua enfocándote en gente y experiencias positivas. Ve y aprecia lo bueno que hay en otras personas.

Las actitudes **positivas** te dan una perspectiva **positiva** en la vida. Es como en la historia del operador del ascensor el cual tarareaba y cantaba un lunes muy temprano por la mañana. Uno de los pasajeros estaba especialmente enfadado por el buen humor del operador y exclamó con enojo, '¿Por qué estás tan contento?' 'Pues, señor,' contestó alegremente, 'es que nunca había vivido antes este día.' (John Maxwell, *La actitud Triunfadora*, p. 43)

¿Qué tipo de cosas te hacen sentir **positivo**?

Pretende que es un día lluvioso y no puedes salir a jugar. ¿Qué harías para crear un día **positivo**?

Quiet

(QUIETUD)

Qq QUIET

Quiet time is a "stop" or a "slow-down" time. **Quiet** time helps us get calm and peaceful inside. It's like Helen, in the book, *Helen and the Great Quiet*, who "had learned how to be so quiet that she even heard the very, very **quiet** sounds of the setting of the sun and the rising of the moon." (Rick Fitzgerald, *Helen and the Great Quiet*, last page.)

How **quiet** can you get?

What's the softest sound you can hear?

Qq QUIETUD

La **quietud** es un momento de tranquilidad es "parar" 'ir más despacio.' Un momento de **quietud** nos ayuda a estar calmados y apacibles por dentro. Es como Elena, en el libro, *Elena y la Gran Quietud*, quien 'aprendió a estar tan **quieta** que podía oír los sonidos más, más tenues, de la puesta del sol y la salida de la luna.' (Rick Fitzgerald, *Helena y la Gran Tranquilidad*, última página.)

¿Qué tan **quieto** puedes quedarte?

¿Cuál es el sonido más tenue que puedes escuchar?

ROOTS
(RAICES)

RR ROOTS

There's a saying that goes something like this: "The two most important things a parent can give a child are **roots** to grow and wings to fly." (Author unknown)

Do you know about your family **roots**?

Who are your grandparents and great-grandparents? Do you know someone who is like a grandparent to you?

Put their names here:

_____

_____

Where do they live?
Did they come from another country?
If so, which one?

_____

What kind of things did they do when they were your age?

What have you learned about them?

What characteristics do you think you inherited from them?

If you had wings to fly:
>   Where would you go?

>   What would you do?

>   What would you be?

RR RAÍCES

Hay un dicho que dice: 'Las dos cosas más importantes que un padre le puede dar a su hijo son **raíces** para crecer y alas para volar.' (Autor desconocido)

¿Sabes cuáles son las **raíces** de tu familia?

¿Quiénes son tus abuelos y tus bisabuelos?

¿Conoces a alguien que sea como un abuelo para ti?

Escribe aquí sus nombres:

_____

_____

¿Dónde viven?
¿Vinieron de otro país?
Si tu respuesta es sí, ¿de que país?

_____

¿Qué tipo de cosas hacían ellos cuando tenían tu edad?

¿Qué has aprendido de ellos?

¿Qué características crees que heredaste de ellos?

Si tuvieras alas para volar:
>   ¿A dónde te gustaría ir?

>   ¿Qué te gustaría hacer?

>   ¿Qué te gustaría ser?

SAFE

(SEGURO)

Ss Safe

Feeling **safe** is a special kind of feeling. There are many ways to feel **safe**. Some people feel **safe** and secure when they are held by someone they love. Listed below are some ways that kids say they feel **safe**:

Katie– "When you are in the car, you put your seatbelt on."

Ryan– "When you cross the street, you look both ways."

Adrian– "When you're at your house, you feel **safe**."

Jaime– "I feel **safe** when I'm asleep in my bed and all the doors are locked."

Erin– "I feel **safe** when my Mom and Dad are home."

Jose– "I feel **safe** when my brother is there."

Liz– "I feel **safe** when I'm with someone older than me."

Sean– "I feel **safe** when I'm around people and I know them."

Jordan– "I feel **safe** when the dog is in the house."

How do you feel **safe**?

Draw your own special picture here.

Ss Seguro

Sentirse **Seguro** es un tipo especial de sentimiento. Hay muchas maneras de sentirse **seguro**. Algunas personas se sientes **seguras** cuando alguien a quien aman los abraza. En la lista de abajo hay algunos ejemplos de las maneras en la que los niños dicen que se sienten **seguros**:

Katie: 'Cuando estás en el carro, y te abrochas el cinturón de seguridad.'

Ryan: 'Cuando cruzas la calle, y miras a ambos lados.'

Adrian: 'Cuando estás en tu casa, te sientes **seguro**.'

Jaime: 'Yo me siento **segura** cuando estoy dormida en mi cama y todas las puertas están cerradas.'

Erin: 'Yo me siento **segura** cuando mi mamá y papá están en casa.'

José: 'Yo me siento **seguro** cuando mi hermano está ahí conmigo.'

Liz: 'Yo me siento **segura** cuando estoy con alguien mayor que yo.'

Sean: 'Me siento **seguro** cuando estoy con gente que conozco.'

Jordan: 'Yo me siento **seguro** cuando el perro está en casa.'

¿Cómo o cuándo te sientes tú **seguro**?

Aquí haz un dibujo que sea especial para ti.

TEAM

(EQUIPO)

Tt Team

Being on a **team** takes cooperation, negotiation, planning, and trust.

Teamwork can be tremendous. Try it!!!

There are baseball teams, soccer teams, basketball teams and teams at work. There are scientific teams that work together to try to solve a problem or make a new discovery. Even a family has to work together as a **team**. A **team** figures out a way to work and play together. A **team** works toward a common goal.

Draw a picture of your **team**.

Tt Equipo

Ser parte de un **equipo** implica cooperación, entendimiento, planeación y confianza.

Trabajar en **equipo** puede ser grandioso. ¡Inténtalo!

Existen equipos de beisbol, equipos de futbol, equipos de baloncesto y equipos en el trabajo. Hay equipos de científicos que trabajan juntos para tratar de resolver algún problema o hacer nuevos descubrimientos. Hasta en una familia tienen que trabajar juntos como un **equipo**. Un **equipo** se las arregla para poder trabajar y jugar juntos. Un **equipo** trabaja hacia una meta común.

Haz un dibujo de tu **equipo**.

UNIQUE

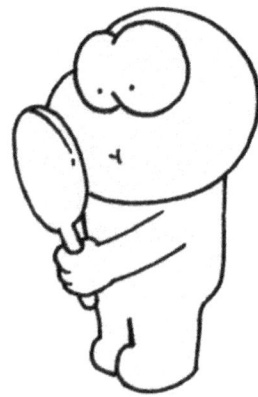

(ÚNICO)

Uu Unique

Each one of us is **unique**. That means that each person is very special. No two people on earth are exactly alike—not even identical twins. That also means that no two people have the same thumb prints or fingerprints—not even identical twins!

Use this space to make your own **unique** thumb print art. Look in a mirror to see that you are **unique**.

Use pictures, colored paper, and colored pencils to make an artistic picture of how **unique** you are. Express yourself.

Uu Único

Cada uno de nosotros es **único**. Eso significa que cada persona es muy especial. No hay dos personas en la tierra que sean exactamente iguales — ni siquiera gemelos idénticos. Lo cual significa que no hay dos personas que tengan las mismas huellas digitales - ¡ni siquiera gemelos idénticos!

Utiliza este espacio para hacer tu propia obra de arte **única** de tu dedo pulgar. Mírate en el espejo para que veas que eres **único**.

Usa dibujos, papel y lápices de color para hacer una obra de arte de cómo eres **único**. Exprésate.

VISUALIZE

(VISUALIZA)

Vv   VISUALIZE

To **visualize** is to think and to create a magical place in your mind. **Visualize** things that you can see, touch, smell, taste and hear. If you close your eyes, what can you **visualize**? Sometimes we **visualize**:

- A beautiful meadow
- A sunny day
- A peaceful world
- Big beautiful clouds
- A world without hunger
- A giant ice cream cone
- A world without pain
- A cuddly puppy

Tell a story or tell someone your story. Draw a picture here about what you **visualize**.

Vv   VISUALIZA

Visualizar es imaginar y crear un lugar mágico en tu mente. **Visualiza** cosas que puedes ver, tocar, oler, probar y oír. ¿Cuándo cierras los ojos, qué puedes **visualizar**? A veces **visualizamos**:

- Un campo hermoso
- Un día soleado
- Un mundo en paz
- Nubes grandes y bonitas
- Un mundo sin hambre
- Un cono de helado gigante
- Un mundo sin dolor
- Un perrito cariñoso

Cuenta una historia o platícale a alguien tú historia. Haz un dibujo aquí sobre lo que **visualizas**.

WISHES

(DESEOS)

Ww Wishes

Wishes are a special kind of thought. Having **wishes** is like having hope for something special. Sometimes **wishes** don't come true, and sometimes they do come true. Sometimes we might have to work hard to make our **wishes** come true.

Wishes are important because they give us hope and something to strive for.

Make a wish. What did you wish for?

Make *more* **wishes**. What are your **wishes**?

Draw one of your **wishes** here.

Ww Deseos

Los **deseos** son un tipo especial de pensamientos. Tener **deseos** es como tener la esperanza de algo muy especial. A veces los **deseos** no se hacen realidad y a veces sí se hacen realidad. Algunas veces tenemos que trabajar duro para que nuestros **deseos** se hagan realidad.

Los **deseos** son importantes porque nos dan esperanza y nos muestran algo porque lo que podemos esforzarnos.

Pide un **deseo**. ¿Qué deseaste?

Pide más **deseos**. ¿Cuáles son tus **deseos**?

Dibuja aquí uno de tus **deseos**.

X-RAY

(RAYOS X.)

Xx X-RAY

An **x-ray** machine can take pictures of the bones and organs inside our bodies. If we break a bone, an **x-ray** will show where and how the bone is broken. This **x-ray** picture will help tell a doctor what to do to help set the bone so that it can heal properly. Special **x-ray** machines can see your organs inside you and can tell if they are healthy.

While **x-ray** machines can see a lot of things inside of you, there are lots of things x-rays can't see. X-rays can't see the things we feel. For instance, when does your heart go pitter-patter with happiness?

Write or draw your answer here.

How does your stomach feel when you are afraid?

Write or draw your answer here.

How does your head feel when you dream big dreams?

Write or draw your answer here.

Xx RAYOS X

Una máquina de **rayos x** puede tomar fotos de nuestros huesos y órganos dentro de nuestro cuerpo. Si nos rompemos un hueso, los **rayos x** nos muestran dónde y cómo está roto nuestro hueso. Esa foto de rayos x le ayuda al doctor a ver cómo va a reponer el hueso para que sane adecuadamente. Las máquinas especiales de **rayos x** pueden ver los órganos dentro de tu cuerpo y decirte si están saludables.

Mientras que las máquinas de **rayos x** pueden ver muchas cosas dentro de ti, hay muchas cosas que los rayos x no pueden ver. Los **rayos x** no pueden ver lo que sentimos. Por ejemplo, ¿cuándo sientes que tu corazón salta de alegría?

Escribe o dibuja aquí tu respuesta.

¿Cómo sientes tu estómago cuando tienes miedo?

Escribe o dibuja aquí tu respuesta.

¿Cómo sientes tu cabeza cuando tienes grandes sueños?

Escribe o dibuja aquí tu respuesta.

(sí)

YES

123

ABC

Yy YES

When you say **yes** to life, you say **yes** to:

> Adventure
> Discovery
> Knowledge
> Learning
> Nature

What would you like to learn? Saying **yes** to learning is power.

What will you become when you say **yes**?

How will you help others?

Ss Sí

Cuando le dices **sí** a la vida, les dices **sí** a:

> La aventura
> El descubrimiento
> La sabiduría
> El aprendizaje
> La naturaleza

¿Qué te gustaría aprender? Decirle **sí** al aprendizaje es poder aprender.

¿Qué podrías lograr al decir **sí**?

¿Cómo podrías ayudar a otros?

ZEST

(ENTUSIASMO)

Zz Zest

When all is said and done, it is the **zest**, the love for life that keeps us all going. Always keep your **zest**!

Draw a picture of yourself being full of **zest**.

Zz Entusiasmo

Cuando todo está dicho y hecho, es el **entusiasmo**, el amor hacia la vida lo que nos mantiene a todos adelante. ¡Mantén siempre tu **entusiasmo**!

Haz un dibujo de ti mismo lleno de **entusiasmo**.

My Family Matters To Me

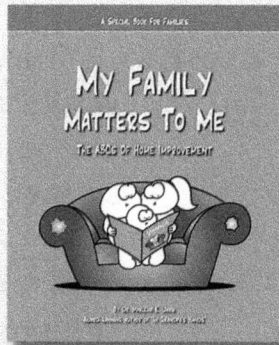

Certificate of Completion

My family finished the book and had fun together!

My name is

_____

My family members' names are

_____

_____

SIGNED _____ DATE _____

For some free stuff and more information, go to the book's web site at
www.MyFamilyMattersToMe.com, or call
1.888.348.0002

MI FAMILIA ME IMPORTA

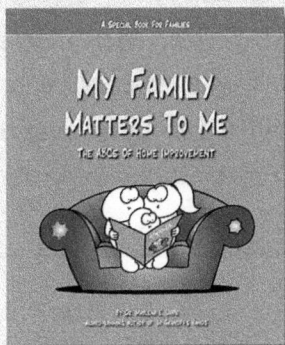

CERTIFICADO DE REALIZACIÓN

¡MI FAMILIA TERMINÓ EL LIBRO Y SE DIVIRTIÓ!!

MI NOMBRE ES

_____

LOS MIEMBROS DE MI FAMILIA SON

_____

_____

FIRMA _____ FECHA _____

Para mayor información y para recibir algunos de los materiales gratuitos visita el cibersitio del libro
www.MyFamilyMattersToMe.com, o llama al
1.888.348.0002

Mi Familia Me Importa
El ABC del Mejoramiento del Hogar

Mi Familia me Importa está diseñado para ayudar a padres de familia y proveedores de cuidado que sienten que no dedican suficiente 'tiempo de calidad' con sus familias. Este libro provee actividades interactivas educativas y divertidas basadas en el abecedario de la "A" a la "Z", y alienta a que todos escriban en el libro, iluminen los dibujos y añadan fotos de su familia. Así que no sólo fomenta la enseñanza del "ABC", sino que también imparte enseñanzas como responsabilidad, honradez y trabajo en equipo. Este libro está especialmente diseñado para niños de 5-10 años, siendo un gran recurso para todos los miembros de la familia para aprender a divertirse juntos.

A diferencia de cualquier otro libro, este libro promueve comprensión y comunicación y ayuda a las familias a apreciar el significado profundo del porque *Mi Familia me Importa*.

————— PRAISE —————

"*Mi Familia me Importa* es una herramienta para nuevos padres de familia y abuelos para entablar comunicación con sus niños de una manera divertida e inofensiva. Éste no es un libro académico sino una dulce guía para fomentar costumbres e interacciones positivas y memorables entre niños y adultos, Lo recomiendo."

—**Delaine Eastin**, exSuperintendente de instrucción Pública de California

"*Mi Familia me Importa* es un enriquecedor juego de ejercicios y puntos de discusión diseñados para incrementar el amor y la atención dentro de la unidad familiar."

—**Jacques S. Benninga**, Ph.D., Director del Bonner Center for Character Education and Citizenship, CSU, Fresno

"Desde hace mucho tiempo tenemos planos de construcción de casas: la Dra. Uhrik nos ha dado los planos para la construcción de un HOGAR. ¡Este es una gran cimiento!"   —**Richard**, Contractor, Papá, Abuelo

"Este libro enseña comunidad, autoestima, valores, liderazgo y fortaleza."
—**Karen**, Hija, Estudiante

"Un libro para ser guardado junto al álbum de fotos familiares y amorosamente pasarlo de generación en generación." —**Loni**, Proprietaria, Mamá, Madrastra

Para adquirir materiales gratuitos de Trabajo Conjunto y Diversión Familiar vaya a: **www.myfamilymatterstome.com**

——— ELOGIOS SOBRE ———

La Dra. Marlena E. Uhrik ha proporcionado programas y servicios para niños y sus familias por más de cuarenta años y ha recibido numerosos reconocimientos locales, estatales y nacionales por su labor en el mejoramiento de la calidad de vida de los niños y sus familias. Ella ha sido reconocida en el Archivo del Congreso de la Casa de Representantes de los EEUU y en 2009 también recibió el Premio Presidencial de Servicio a los EEUU por su extenso y comprometido trabajo comunitario.

Para conocer más sobre formas de participación y como puede generar cambios en su comunidad visite

www.allwayslearning.biz

Una porción de las ganancias por la venta de este libro será distribuida para ayudar a alimentar niños hambrientos.

PUBLICADO POR ALL WAYS LEARNING, LLC., WWW.ALLWAYSLEARNING.BIZ